American Lives

Sojourner Truth

Jennifer Blizin Gillis

Heinemann Library
Chicago, Illinois

Designed by Q2A Creative

Printed in China by WKT Limited

10 09 08 07 06
10 9 8 7 6 5 4 3 2 1

Library of Congress Cataloging-in-Publication Data
Gillis, Jennifer Blizin, 1950-
  Sojourner Truth/Jennifer Blizin Gillis.
    p. cm.–(American lives)
  Includes bibliographical references and index.
  ISBN 1-4034-6981-4 (hc)–ISBN 1-4034-6988-1
    (pb)

  1. Truth, Sojourner, d. 1883–Juvenile literature.
2. African American abolitionists–Biography–
Juvenile literature. 3. African American women–
Biography–Juvenile literature. 4. Abolitionists–
United States–Biography–Juvenile literature.
5. Social reformers–United States–Biography–
Juvenile literature. I. Title. II. Series: American
lives (Heinemann Library (Firm))

E185.97.T8G55 2006
306.3'62'092–dc22

2005010325

Acknowledgments
The author and publishers are grateful to the following for permission to reproduce copyright material:

Bridgeman Art Library/Private Collection/Bourne Gallery, Reigate p. **9**; Corbis pp. **7** (Leonard de Selva), **8**, **17**, **24**, **27**; Corbis/Bettmann pp. **19**, **26**; Corbis/Photo Collection Alexander Alland, Sr. p. **16**; Corbis/Stapleton Collection p. **13**; Getty Images/Hulton Archive pp. **11**, **23**; Getty Images/Hulton Archive/MPI p. **28**; Granger Collection pp. **4**, **12**, **14**, **15**, **18**, **20**, **25**; Jay Warren p. **5**; New York Public Library p. **6**; State Archives of Michigan pp. **21**, **22**, **29**; The Image Works p.**10** (Suzanne Taetzsch).

Cover photograph of Sojourner Truth in 1864 reproduced with permission of the Granger Collection.

Every effort has been made to contact copyright holders of any material reproduced in this book. Any omissions will be rectified in subsequent printings if notice is given to the publisher.

Some words are shown in bold, **like this**. You can find out what they mean by looking in the glossary.

Contents

"I Want to Ride!"

In 1865, an African-American woman waited for a **streetcar** in Washington, D.C. Horses pulled the streetcar closer. The old woman waved for it to stop. But it did not slow down. She called out, "I want to ride! I want to ride!" When the streetcar finally stopped, the driver told the woman she had to sit near the horses with the other African Americans. The woman refused. "I know my rights," she said, as she took her seat among the white passengers.

This is a photo of Sojourner Truth when she was about 67 years old.

This statue of Sojourner Truth is in Florence, Massachusetts.

Another day, the woman got on a different streetcar. The driver tried to shove her off, hurting her shoulder. The woman took the driver to court. She won her case and the driver lost his job.

The woman was Sojourner Truth. Born a slave, she spent much of her life speaking out for equal rights for African Americans and women. Nearly 100 years later, **activists** called "freedom riders" would take buses to the South to work for the same things. Sojourner was the first freedom rider.

Childhood

The child who became Sojourner Truth was born around 1797 in Hurley, New York. Her parents, James and Betsey, named her Isabella Baumfree. They were slaves who belonged to a Dutch farmer.

Isabella was one of ten children. Some of her brothers and sisters had already been sold away from the family. The slaveowner was not cruel, but he thought of Isabella's family as property, not people. The home he gave them was a cold basement with a dirt floor.

Slaves were often taken many miles by boat and train to their new owners.

The Life of Sojourner Truth

1797	1815	1826	1843
Isabella Baumfree born	*Isabella marries, about 1815*	*Isabella wins court case to get her son Peter back*	*Changes name to "Sojourner Truth"*

Slaves were sold at auctions. Some slaves never saw their families again.

Isabella's mother was very religious. She taught Isabella that God would always listen to her prayers. Although Isabella never learned to read or write, she learned most of the Bible by heart.

When Isabella was about nine years old, she was sold to new owners. Because her father was sick, Isabella's parents were freed and allowed to stay on the old farm.

1845-60s	1864	1868-1870s	1883
Travels and speaks out against slavery	*Meets President Abraham Lincoln*	*Tries to get free land for African Americans*	*Dies November 26, 1883*

Hard Times

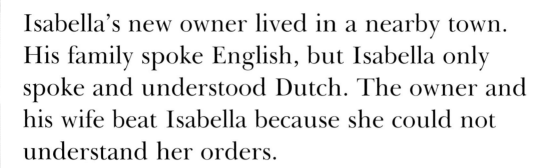

Isabella's new owner lived in a nearby town. His family spoke English, but Isabella only spoke and understood Dutch. The owner and his wife beat Isabella because she could not understand her orders.

Living in the cold basement had ruined her parents' health. Isabella's mother died very suddenly. When she went to her mother's funeral, Isabella found that her father was very sick, too.

Isabella could not stay to help her father. She had to go back to her new owner. One day, he beat her very badly. She prayed for her father to come get her.

Some owners were very cruel to their slaves. They could beat or mistreat them for any reason at all.

Working in a tavern was hard work, but it helped Isabella learn English.

Isabella's father had heard about the beatings. Even though he was sick, he tried to help her. He talked a man named Martin Schryver into buying his daughter.

The Schryvers owned a farm and a **tavern**. They were not cruel, but they were lazy and sloppy. Isabella was their only slave. She had to do most of the work. She took care of the crops and worked in the tavern. She learned how to speak English.

Isabella was about twelve years old when she heard that her father had died. Unable to work anymore, he had starved to death.

Love and Marriage

This picture shows farmland near New Paltz, New York today.

After about two years, the Schryvers sold Isabella to a farmer named Dumont. She soon fell in love with a slave from another farm. His name was Robert. Isabella and Robert wanted to marry, but Robert's owner would not allow it.

Robert's owner found out that he was still visiting Isabella. This made him angry. One day, Robert's owner followed him to the Dumonts'. When Robert got to the Dumonts', his owner beat Robert nearly to death. Robert never visited Isabella again. Robert's owner made him marry a slave from his own farm.

Isabella's Children

Isabella and Thomas had four children named Diana, Elizabeth, Peter, and Sophia.

Isabella married an older slave named Thomas. He had been married twice before, but his wives had been sold to new owners.

When she was about 20 years old, Isabella got good news. New York passed a law saying slaves born before 1799 would be freed in 1827. Dumont told her that if she worked really hard, he would free her a year early. For two years, Isabella did extra work. The other slaves laughed at her. They said their owner would never free her.

This old drawing shows a slave wedding. Since slaves were property, any children they had belonged to the slaveowner.

Runaway!

Around her 29th birthday, Isabella asked Dumont to set her free. He refused, saying she had not worked hard enough. Soon after, Isabella took her baby Sophia and ran away. She left her husband and other children behind.

A **Quaker** family named the Van Wagenens took Isabella in. They paid Isabella's owner to set her free.

Slaves who ran away were in great danger. If they were caught escaping, their owners could punish them severely.

Quakers believed in living simply. Their clothes were old-fashioned and plain. Their religion taught that everyone was equal, so they believed that slavery was wrong.

Then, Isabella heard that her five-year-old son, Peter, was sold to a slaveowner in Alabama. There were no laws against slavery there. Isabella worried Peter might never be free. It was against the law for a slave to be taken to another state. Isabella went to court to rescue Peter. She knew she would have to spend a lot of time in court. She left baby Sophia with the Van Wagenens.

When the judge heard Isabella's case, he made the slaveowner bring Peter back. Isabella said, "I felt so tall within—I felt as though the power of a nation was with me!" Isabella and Peter lived with the Van Wagenens for two years.

On Her Own

This is how New York City looked when Isabella lived there.

When Isabella was about 31 years old, she moved to New York City. She went to work as a servant in the homes of wealthy families. Peter went into a school to learn to be a sailor.

In New York, Isabella joined the Zion African Church. The people who went there often testified, or spoke out during the church service, about their religious feelings. Isabella became known as a good speaker who could **recite** parts of the Bible from memory.

In her free time, Isabella helped out in a shelter for homeless women. A minister named Elijah Pierson ran it. When his wife died, he decided to start a **religious community** in the country. Isabella decided to move there.

New Religions

In the 1800s, people became interested in many new religions. People sometimes started farms, or communities, where believers could live, work, and worship together.

These people are called Shakers. They made and sold furniture to make money for their religious community.

A New Name

One summer, Isabella heard God telling her to travel and talk to people about religion. Right away, she left her job and took a ferry to Long Island, New York. She walked and prayed. She believed that God wanted her to change her name to *Sojourner,* meaning traveler. She changed her last name to *Truth.*

Sojourner Truth walked all over Long Island. In villages and on farms, she preached and **recited** parts of the Bible. She worked in exchange for food and a place to sleep.

This old photograph shows a village on Long Island in the 1900s.

After Frederick Douglass was freed, he spent the rest of his life fighting first for the end of slavery and then to better the lives of freed slaves.

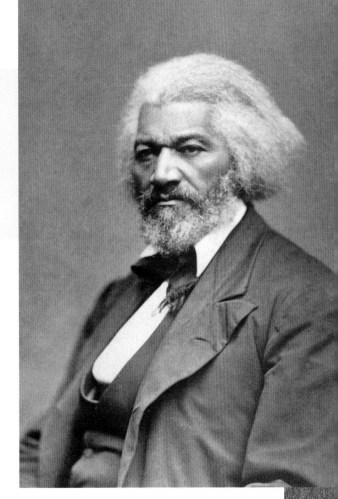

At the end of the summer, Sojourner traveled to Northampton, Massachusetts. At the age of 46, she joined another religious community. The people there were **abolitionists** who wanted to abolish, or end, slavery. They also wanted equal rights for women. Isabella met Frederick Douglass. He was a freed slave and a famous abolitionist.

When the religious community broke up, Sojourner stayed nearby to work as a housekeeper. She became very involved in the work the abolitionists were doing to end slavery in the South.

Speaking Out

Sojourner dressed in **Quaker**-style clothes. She was nearly six feet tall. She was only 53 when this picture was taken, but she looked older because she had lived a hard life.

Sojourner began speaking at **abolitionist** and women's rights meetings. Some friends lent her a horse and buggy so she could travel more easily. Though she was not educated, Sojourner was a powerful speaker. She used sayings and stories to make people remember her speeches.

One of Sojourner's white friends, Olive Gilbert, helped her write a book about her life. The book was called *The Narrative of Sojourner Truth*.

Sojourner sold copies of her book at abolitionist meetings and **conferences** on women's rights. When she was 55, she went to a national women's conference. She was surprised that all of the speakers were men.

On the second day of the conference, Sojourner stood and began to speak. She told the men that they should not be afraid to let women have equal rights. She said, "I have as much muscle as any man, and can do as much work as any man . . . and aren't I a woman?" People at the conference loved her speech.

This drawing shows an anti-slavery meeting.

Troubled Times

The United States was becoming divided over slavery. Slavery was now against the law in northern states. But people in southern states were still allowed to own slaves. As new states joined the country, fights broke out over whether people could own slaves there.

Around this time, an author named Harriet Beecher Stowe wrote a best-selling book called *Uncle Tom's Cabin*. It turned thousands of people against slavery. Harriet met Sojourner and was so impressed that she wrote an **essay** telling people to read Sojourner's book. This helped Sojourner become famous.

Uncle Tom's Cabin told the story of an old slave named Tom, a young slave named Topsy, and their cruel boss Simon Legree.

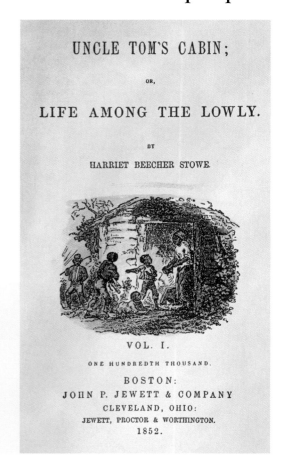

UNCLE TOM'S CABIN;

OR,

LIFE AMONG THE LOWLY.

BY

HARRIET BEECHER STOWE.

VOL. I.

ONE HUNDREDTH THOUSAND.

BOSTON:
JOHN P. JEWETT & COMPANY
CLEVELAND, OHIO:
JEWETT, PROCTOR & WORTHINGTON.
1852.

This is a poster advertizing one of Sojourner's lectures.

In 1861, the **Civil War** began. Sojourner worried that slavery would be allowed in every state if the South won the war. At the age of 60, she began to travel and speak out for the **Union**.

She traveled through Illinois and Iowa. People who wanted slavery yelled at and mistreated her. At that time it was against the law for freed black people to enter Indiana. When she went there to speak, Sojourner was arrested and put in jail. Another time, a crowd of men shoved her around and she was badly hurt. She walked with a cane for the rest of her life. Still, she spoke out against slavery.

Meeting the President

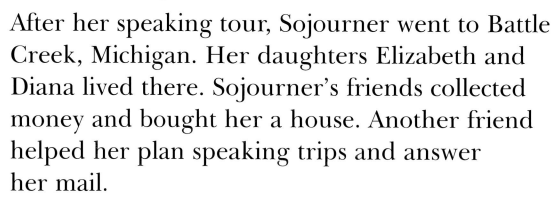

After her speaking tour, Sojourner went to Battle Creek, Michigan. Her daughters Elizabeth and Diana lived there. Sojourner's friends collected money and bought her a house. Another friend helped her plan speaking trips and answer her mail.

During the **Civil War**, Harriet Beecher Stowe published an article about meeting Sojourner. This made Sojourner the most well-known African-American woman in the country.

During the war, Sojourner made speeches to many young African-American men. Because of her, many of them joined the **Union** army to fight against the South.

This is how Battle Creek looked in the 1800s.

During the Civil War, Abraham Lincoln was President of the United States. Sojourner wanted to meet this man who had ended slavery. She took a train to Washington, D.C. Along the way, she stopped to make speeches.

President Lincoln met with her at the White House. He signed Sojourner's *Book of Life*. This was a special scrapbook filled with letters and signatures from famous people.

Sojourner met with President Lincoln to thank him for the Emancipation Proclamation, a law that made slavery illegal.

23

Washington, D.C.

Slavery was against the law in Washington, D.C., so the town was full of escaped and freed slaves. Living conditions were very hard for them. Many of them lived in shacks near the U.S. Capitol. Slavecatchers raided the shacks, kidnapping people and taking them to the South so they could get money.

Sojourner decided to stay and help take care of people who had been slaves. She also helped raise money to buy supplies for African-American soldiers.

Many people who had been slaves lived in camps like this one in Arlington, Virginia.

President Lincoln was shot while he watched a play at a theater in Washington, D.C.

For a while, Sojourner worked at a camp for freed slaves in Virginia. She tried to help them find jobs and places to live. Then, she got a government job. She helped run a hospital for freed slaves in Washington, D.C.

President Lincoln was killed in April, 1865. The **Civil War** ended soon after. The North—and the **Union**—had won. There would be no more slavery in the United States.

Go West!

For a time after the **Civil War**, soldiers stayed in the South to make sure that African Americans were not mistreated. **Congress** changed the **Constitution** to give African Americans equal rights.

Some southern cities and states were against these changes. They began to make rules and pass **Jim Crow laws** to keep blacks and whites apart. Washington, D.C. was not a southern city, but the **streetcar** company would not let black and white passengers ride together. Sojourner took them to court. The judge ruled that African Americans could ride in the same cars as white passengers.

Sojourner refused to ride in "Jim Crow" cars. Because of her, the streetcar company finally allowed black and white passengers to ride together.

Ulysses S. Grant was the leader of the Union army during the Civil War. He would go on to become President of the United States.

When Sojourner was about 71 years old, she asked the government to give free land to anyone who had been a slave. At this time, places like Oregon, Nebraska, and North and South Dakota were just becoming states. There was plenty of open land there.

Sojourner met with members of Congress about her plan. They told her to give them a **petition**, or paper signed by many people, asking them to do this. Sojourner paid for petitions to be printed. She traveled for a year, collecting thousands of signatures.

Last Years

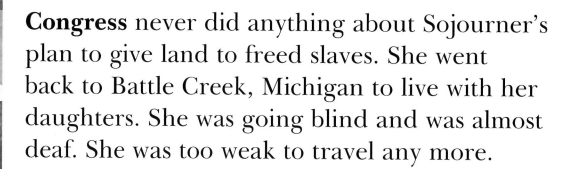

Congress never did anything about Sojourner's plan to give land to freed slaves. She went back to Battle Creek, Michigan to live with her daughters. She was going blind and was almost deaf. She was too weak to travel any more.

In the South, conditions were getting worse for African Americans. A new president called home the soldiers who had stayed in the South after the **Civil War**. He did not think anyone should have to protect the rights of African Americans. Then, the government let each state decide whether African Americans could vote. Most southern states passed more **Jim Crow laws** to keep African Americans from voting.

In the late 1800s, groups like the Ku Klux Klan tried to frighten African Americans to keep them apart from white people and to stop them from voting. In many states, African Americans did not vote again until the mid-1960s.

Sojourner Truth is buried in Battle Creek, Michigan.

Sojourner had many friends who came to visit her and her daughters. Her old friend Olive Gilbert visited her, too. Although she was getting sicker, Sojourner did not complain. She said, "I am above 80 years old; it is about time for me to be going. I have been 40 years a slave and 40 years free, and would be here 40 more years to have equal rights for all."

Sojourner died at home on November 26, 1883. She was about 86 years old. More than 1,000 people came to her funeral. Many of them were **activists** who had worked with her for equal rights.

Glossary

abolitionist person who worked to end slavery

activist person who takes action to change things

Civil War war that lasted from 1861 to 1865 in which the northern states fought against southern states

conference large meeting that lasts several days

Congress group of men and women who make the laws for the United States

Constitution important paper that explains how the government works and the rights that people have in the United States

essay writing in which a person gives his or her opinion about something

Jim Crow laws unfair rules to keep black and white people apart. They were put in place in some states after slavery ended.

petition paper that has been signed by many people who want to change something

Quaker Christian religion that says every person must worship God in his or her own way and that everyone is equal

recite speaking something, like a book or a poem, from memory and in front of people

religious community farm or village in which people live, work, and worship together

streetcar kind of train that took people around towns

tavern public house that serves food and drink

30 **Union** name for the states that remained loyal to the U.S. Government during the Civil War

More Books to Read

Frost, Helen. *Sojourner Truth*. Mankato, MN: Capstone Press, 2003.

Mattern, Joanne: *Sojourner Truth: Early Abolitionist*. New York: Rosen, 2003.

Spinale, Laura. *Sojourner Truth*. Chanhassen, MN: The Child's World, 1999.

Place to Visit

The National Civil Rights Museum
450 Mulberry Street
Memphis, TN
(901) 521-9699

Index